Living *with* Stress

By Judy Murphy

GRASS ROOTS PRESS
Edmonton, Alberta

Second Printing 2009

Living with Stress is published by

Grass Roots Press
A division of Literacy Services of Canada Ltd.
www.grassrootsbooks.net

Author: Judy Murphy
Content consultant: Sandra Schwanke
Editor: Leslie Dawson and Pat Campbell
Copy editor: Judith Tomlinson
Illustrator: Val Lawton
Photographer: Judy Murphy
Book design: Lara Minja, Lime Design Inc.
Printing: McCallum Printing Group Inc.

We acknowledge the financial support of the Government of Canada through the Book Publishing Industry Development Program (BPIDP) for our publishing activities.

We acknowledge the support of the Alberta Foundation for the Arts for our publishing programs.

We acknowledge funding from the National Literacy Secretariat, Human Resources and Skills Development Canada.

The publisher has made efforts to ensure that the information in this book is accurate and up-to-date. The book cannot replace the services of a doctor or other health worker. If you think that you have a medical problem, be sure to get advice from a trained health-care worker.

Library and Archives Canada Cataloguing in Publication

Murphy, Judy, 1942
Living with stress / by Judy Murphy; illustrated by Val Lawton.

ISBN 1-894593-36-7

1. Readers for new literates. 2. Stress (Psychology).
I. Lawton, Valerie II. Title.

PE1126.N43M87 2005 428.6'2 C2005-904256-7

Printed in Canada

Table of Contents

Thank You

Many people helped to put this book together.

Five focus groups were organized in Alberta to share ideas and knowledge about the content and appearance of the books in the Easy-to-Read Health Series. I wish to give special thanks to participants in Alberta's literacy and community programs. Many people took part. These people gave permission to print their names:

Amanda Akkerman
Ann
Bill Littlejohn
C. Kameyosit
C. Monias
Darell Demeria
Dave A. Rasmden
Debbie Longo
Della Akkerman
Delia Manychief
Denise Banack
Dione Dubois
Elvis Quintal
Ernie Lonewolf
Fred Cazon
Glen Dumont
Gloria Herbert
Hazel
Helen
I.A. Butler
Iwalani A. Post
Ive
Jeanne Longo
Jim Judd
Jung Zheng
Kathy Helms
L. Miskenack
Lynne Gendron
Lynne W.
Liz
Mark Garbutt
Marvin Mochid
Matthew Ivan
Mavis Prevost
Monica Catellier
Nora Potts
Priscilla Wallin
Rachel Kretz
Robert Desjarlais
Shawn Worbs
Sherien Lo
Susan Murray
Terri Schneider
V. Faithful

I thank those who facilitated the focus groups and the programs and agencies that hosted them: Dani Ducross, Coordinator of Adult Literacy Program in Lacombe; Anna Reitman, Coordinator of Edmonton John Howard Society's Alternative Learning Program; Berniece Gowan and Sandra Loschnig, focus group facilitators at Calgary Elizabeth Fry Society; and Vesna Kavaz, Coordinator, Literacy Program in Athabasca.

Women at Elizabeth Fry Society of Edmonton met with me to say what information should be in *Living with Stress.* I thank

Cece
Corinne Houle
Kuna Ulch
Melissa R. Paquette
Rena Ahnassay
Shannon Droeske
Tania L. Jorgensen

Participants in Edmonton John Howard's Alternative Learning Program, Elizabeth Fry Society of Edmonton's Changing Paths Program, and The Learning Centre Literacy Association wrote stories about stressful times in their lives. I thank the following for sharing their stories in this book:

Cathy Cumby
Cindy Lingrell
Glen Dumont
Jennifer Ellen Wood
Lillian Gallant
Sheri Morely
W.W.W.

Women in the Women's Health Group at Boyle McCauley Health Centre took part in a workshop on *Living with Stress*. They tried out some ways to reduce stress suggested in this book. They gave helpful feedback on the exercises. I thank Esther Stocker who organized the group and all those who participated in it.

The executive staff members at Boyle McCauley Health Centre, hosts of the Easy-to-Read Health Series project, have been enthusiastic and avid supporters. I thank Cecilia Blasetti, Colleen Novotny, and Wendy Kalamar.

The project has been guided by an Advisory Committee. Each member has given her time and knowledge to guide this project and the first book. I thank Marg Budd, Tobacco Reductionist Coordinator, Capital Health; Pat Campbell, President of Grass Roots Press; Ann Goldblatt, Project Evaluator; Margaret McGeough and Jackie Norman, Coordinators of Changing Paths, Elizabeth Fry Society of Edmonton; Colleen Novotny, Coordinator, Internal Operations, Boyle McCauley Health Centre; and Sandra Schwanke, Psychologist (Alberta).

I thank the project funders, National Literacy Secretariat, Human Resources and Skills Development Canada, for its support.

Thank You!

Judy Murphy
Project Manager and Author
Easy-to-Read Health Series

(Welcome to the stress and relaxation book!

We all feel stressed at one time or another. Stress is part of our day-to-day lives. When hard things happen to us, we usually notice stress right away. Good things cause stress, too. The ideas in this book will help you to manage stress.

This book will help you to understand three things:

- stress and what causes it,
- the way stress makes us feel in our minds and bodies,
- ways to manage stress and feel more relaxed and calm.

✤ **food for thought**

The American Academy of Family Physicians states that about two-thirds of all visits to the family doctor are stress-related.

This book also answers these questions:

- What is stress and what makes us stressed?
- How do we feel when stressed?
- What does stress do to our bodies?
- How do we behave when stressed?
- What can we do to feel less stressed?
- What if we feel too much stress?
- How do we know if our children are stressed?
- What can we do to help our children?

Stress is...

- a leaf tossed in the wind.
- a splinter in my thumb.
- a huge crack in the sidewalk.
- fingernails scraping across the blackboard.
- a train wreck.
- an elastic band stretching.
- a rainstorm coming down.

—Participants in a creative writing class at The Learning Centre Literacy Association

1 Naming Stressors in Our Lives

What is stress?

Stress is a response to something that we think is a threat or challenge. It is also a response to anything that is new or different.

People respond to stress in different ways. Some people feel angry, tense, depressed, or too excited. This type of response is bad for the health. Other people respond by getting more energy to achieve goals. They can use this energy to do such things as finish school. This type of response is good for our health. The way we respond to the changes in our lives can either help or harm us.

Too much stress causes health problems. **Too little** stress makes us bored with our lives. We need to find a balance between feeling too much and too little stress.

I'm writing in the creative writing class right now. I'm feeling stress as I'm having a hard time thinking about what to write.

I get a lot of stress by writing things on paper and using my brain a lot. It is frustrating to make sure that my words are spelled right and that my sentences sound good. Sometimes I feel that I don't want to write anymore as I'm having a hard time trying to think… how to start my sentence. (It is very stressful.)

—Sheri Morley

What causes stress?

It is important to figure out the things that make you feel stressed. Both good and bad experiences can stress you. These experiences or events are called **stressors.** You can lower stress by becoming more aware of the stressors in your life.

✤ **food for thought**

A journey of a thousand miles begins with a single step.

—Confucius

Lots of things make us feel stressed. There are different kinds of stressors. What is stressful for one person might not bother someone else. When we worry about our stressors, we feel even more anxious and stressed. Worrying about things can make you tired.

Each of us worries about different things. For example, you might be stressed when you are late to meet a friend for coffee. Your friend might not mind at all. Your friend might worry about her teenaged children and how they are behaving. Someone else might worry about walking home from work late at night. Or, she might be afraid of being abused by a partner. Many people worry about paying bills.

Types of stressors

Different groups of stressors are on pages 13 and 14.[1]
Check off the stressors in your life.

Stressors in my life

Finances

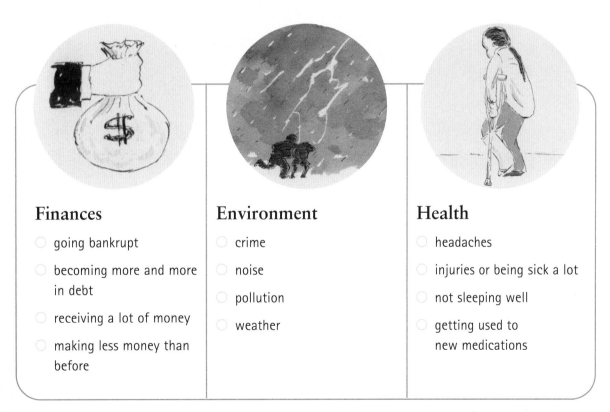

- ○ going bankrupt
- ○ becoming more and more in debt
- ○ receiving a lot of money
- ○ making less money than before

Environment

- ○ crime
- ○ noise
- ○ pollution
- ○ weather

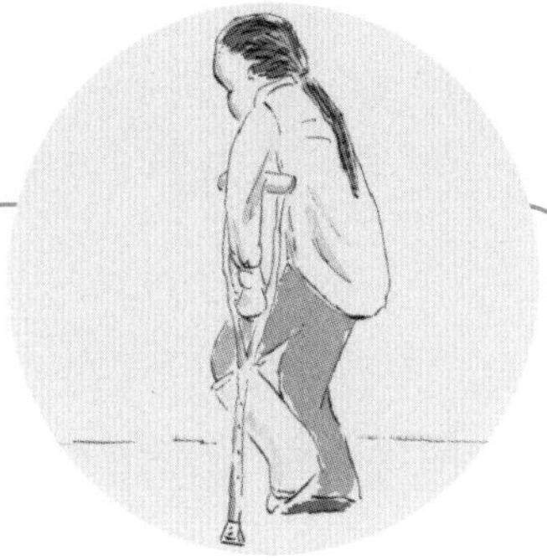

Health

- ○ headaches
- ○ injuries or being sick a lot
- ○ not sleeping well
- ○ getting used to new medications

Stressors in my life

Day-to-Day

- having problems with child care
- forgetting or losing something
- waiting in lines
- having to miss school to pick up medications

Family

- arguments with partner or children
- death of someone close
- drinking or drug problems
- problems with children

Work or School

- having to take a lot of buses to get to work or school
- being fired or asked to leave school
- not getting positive feedback
- going back to school

What stresses you?

On the left below, list important things that stress you. To the right, write what kind of stressor it is (finances, environment, health, day-to-day, family, or work/school).

Two examples will help start you off.

What stresses me	Kind of stress
Missing the bus	Day-to-day
Having fights with my partner	Family

My life was always stressful until I came to the city.

On the farm my parents had no feeling for me. They didn't want a daughter. So I was considered extra baggage. I had to clean up after everybody else, make meals, and look after the babies she had after me. They convinced me I was retarded and took me out of school early. For years I languished on the farm, took their mental abuse and beatings. Finally at age nineteen I married the first guy that asked me. He turned out to be an alcoholic and mental abuser.

PAGE 16 >

Acute and chronic stressors

> Finally the stress got the best of me and I tried suicide. I finally got help at the University of Alberta, and I can deal with stress most of the time with the help of a good psychiatrist. There have been ups and downs, but I have become stronger. I have a new life in Edmonton. I have some great friends I love dearly. Life is good.
>
> I've come to [The Learning] Centre, and I know I am not mentally challenged. I can climb mountains no matter what.
>
> —Cindy Lingrell

Acute stressors last a short time. For example, feeling hungry, writing an exam for your high school equivalency (GED), or having an argument are acute stressors. The stress doesn't last long. The stress level in our bodies returns to normal a short time after the stressing event is over. It usually takes 5 to 30 minutes to lower our stress level.

Chronic stressors last a long time. Chronic stressors are things like not having a place to live or being out of work. Problems with your partner or children, loneliness, and money problems are also chronic. This kind of stress lasts longer than the acute kind—weeks, months, years, or longer. It can make us feel restless, angry, depressed, worried or numb. Chronic stress will cause poor physical health and illnesses, anything from having a lot of colds to cancer.

How Much Stress Do We Have?

You are more likely to get ill if you have lots of stressful changes in one year. It is important to be aware of the stressors in your life. That way you can do something to feel less stressed.

When I went to the provincial literacy conference last year, my apartment was broken into and something very special to me was taken. I got back some things but not everything. I went through a rough time. It was an awful feeling walking into my apartment and seeing things gone that meant so much to me. I called the police but they didn't do too much either. I won an award from Canada Post and a computer. I don't have the computer now as that was stolen and I never got it back.

–L.G.

The Stress Values Chart

This chart will help you learn how much stress you face in your life.

STEP 1: On the left, check off the stressors you have had in the last year. Have you had stressors that are not listed here? Write them down at the bottom of the chart. It is important to know what causes you stress.

The *value* (on the right) says how important that stressor is for you. For example, you will feel more stress if you get a divorce (stress value is 78) than if you get a ticket for disturbing the peace (stress value is 12).

STEP 2: On the right, write down all the stress values for the items you have checked. If a stressor happened more than once, then count it again.

PAGE 18 >

STEP 3: Add up all these values and write down the total under "Your total stress value."

The higher your total is, the higher your chances of getting sick from stress.

Stress Values Chart[2]

✓	Event	Stress values	Your stress values
	death of partner	100	
	divorce	73	
	separating from a partner	65	
	serving time in jail	63	
	death of close family member	63	
	having an injury or illness	53	
	getting married	50	
	getting fired from work	47	
	getting back together with a partner	45	
	retirement	45	
	change in family member's health	44	
	pregnancy	40	

✓	Event	Stress values	Your stress values
	sex problems	39	
	adding a family member	39	
	change in what you do at work	39	
	change in financial level	38	
	death of a close friend	37	
	change to a new kind of work	36	
	change in number of arguments with your partner	35	
	debt over $10,000	31	
	foreclosure of a loan	30	
	change in work duties	29	
	child leaving home	29	
	trouble with in-laws	29	
	outstanding personal success	29	
	partner begins or stops work	28	
	starting or finishing school	26	
	change in living conditions	26	
	change in personal habits	25	
	trouble with your boss	24	
	change in work hours	23	

PAGE 20 >

Stress Values Chart[2]

✓	Event	Stress values	Your stress values
	moving to another place to live	20	
	change in schools	20	
	change in recreation habits	20	
	change in church activities	19	
	change in social activities	18	
	debt less than $10,000	18	
	change in sleeping habits	17	
	change in number of family get-togethers	16	
	change in eating habits	15	
	vacation	14	
	Christmas holiday	13	
	minor trouble with the law (traffic tickets, disturbing the peace)	12	
			Your total stress value:

How high is your stress?

150-199 or less:	You are doing well.
200-299:	You are feeling stressed. You need to find ways to calm yourself and relax.
300 or more:	You are feeling a lot of stress. You need to find ways to manage your stress.

Remember!! Information is power. You can do many things to keep healthy and well. That's what this book is about.

Now you know what stress is and what causes your stress. Next, you need to know what stress does to you.

food for thought

"Life is about 20% in what happens to us and 80% in the way we respond to crisis."

- Ted Engstrom

(2 Responding to Stress

The body/mind connection

How do you respond to stress? That's the most important thing to figure out. Maybe you're one of those people who handle stress really well. These people are said to be "stress-hardy." Others worry all the time and become more stressed.

When we decide something is stressful, our bodies can go into "fight or flight." This is called a **stress response.** During this response

- our heart rates go faster.
- our blood pressure goes up.
- our breathing speeds up.
- our muscles tense.
- we have lots of energy.

✤ **food for thought**

"Stress is the spice of life."

- Hans Selye

After the stress is over, our bodies feel tired and then quickly go back to normal. This is called the relaxation response. If we keep worrying and our stress continues, our bodies stay in the "fight or flight" mode. We become tired and sick.

✤ **food for thought**

Do not anticipate trouble or worry about what may never happen. Keep in the sunlight.

—Ben Franklin

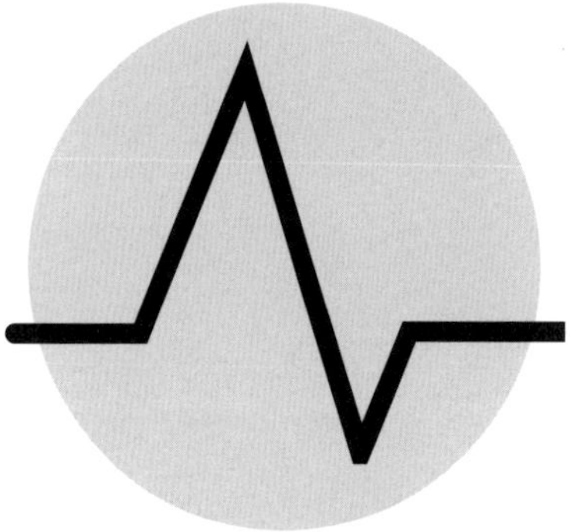

Acute Stress Pattern

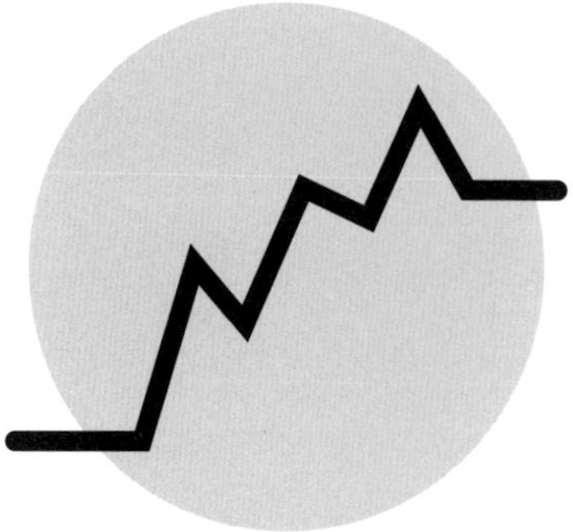

Chronic Stress Pattern

Symptoms of Stress

In order to reduce and manage stress, you need to be aware of your stressors and your symptoms—your signs of stress. You've had a chance to figure out your stressors. Here is an activity to help you identify symptoms of stress.

Body check-in

Let's take a look at how stress affects your body. Put a check beside the symptoms you get when you feel stressed.

How I respond to stress

These are things that happen to my body.

- ◯ My allergies get worse.
- ◯ I get tired.
- ◯ I get back pain.
- ◯ I feel chest pains.
- ◯ I get clammy hands.
- ◯ I get a fluttering heart.
- ◯ I get butterflies in my stomach.
- ◯ I feel weak all over.
- ◯ I get headaches.
- ◯ I feel restless.
- ◯ I get sweaty all over.

Does your body respond in other ways?

____

How I respond to stress

These are some of the things I do.

- ○ I use more alcohol, tobacco, or other drugs.
- ○ I argue more with my friends and partner.
- ○ I don't care how I look anymore.
- ○ I cry easily.
- ○ I am late for school and appointments.
- ○ I withdraw from family and friends.
- ○ I forget stuff easily.
- ○ I have a hard time concentrating.

Do you notice other changes?

____

____

____

____

____

____

____

Mind check-in

Stress changes the way we think and feel. Remember that the body and mind are closely connected.

What I think and feel under stress

Under stress, some things I think are…

- ○ I can't do it.
- ○ What if I make a fool of myself?
- ○ What if someone is hurt, sick, fired, etc.?
- ○ I don't have a problem.
- ○ I can't make up my mind.

Do you have any other thoughts?

____

____

____

____

What I think and feel under stress

Under stress, some things I feel are...

- ◯ I'm angry.
- ◯ I'm fearful.
- ◯ I'm on edge.
- ◯ I feel panic setting in.
- ◯ I'm worried most of the time.
- ◯ I feel depressed.

Do you get other feelings when stressed?

It is a good idea to look at the symptoms of stress that bother us. We can get used to feeling and thinking in these ways. Unless we stop and notice, we may not even know we are under stress.

When I was fourteen and going to school, I was wearing a body brace. The students always would tease me, pick on me and put me down with words so that started my stress to rise very fast, furious.

—W.W.W.

Now we are aware of what stress is, what causes our stress, and our symptoms of stress. Next, we can do something about it. Yoga is a very old science that teaches us about well-being. It teaches that three things are connected—mind, body, and breath. For example, by changing how we think, we will see changes in the other two—our breath and body. If we calm our breath, the body and mind will relax. All three—mind, body, and breath—affect how we feel.

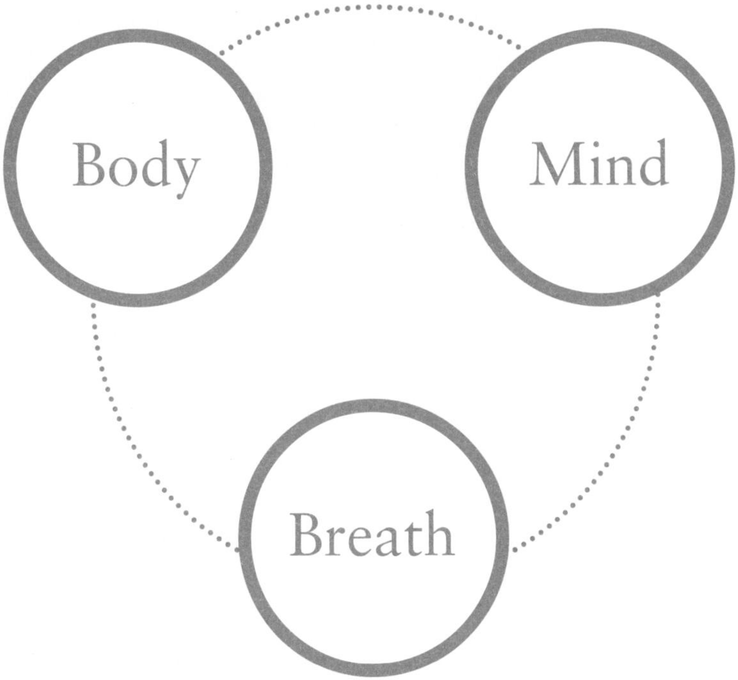

The next three chapters are *Calming our Bodies*, *Calming our Breath*, and *Calming our Minds*. They tell us things we can do to manage our stress.

✤ **food for thought**

There's no better way to energize your body, mind, and spirit than by taking care of yourself.

—Stephanie Tourles

When I was 21 I thought my world would change for the better. Boy was I wrong! I ended up raising my daughter on my own when my husband left me. Which meant a commitment from me to stay strong, no matter what. So I did. I started spending money I didn't have and limited my social life.

On a daily basis I wake up at six, make two lunches, get dressed, wake my daughter, and go off to school. I arrive home around 5 p.m. Supper must be made, and homework done, hers and mine. There's laundry to be done, dishes, and housework. I must squeeze in quality time—never mind my time now, it doesn't matter now. I fall asleep around 10 pm and try to relax and fall asleep for tomorrow I do it all again. Life is hard being a single mother, but I wouldn't trade it in for anything in the world.

—Cathy Cumby

✤ **food for thought**

The sun shines not on us, but in us.

—John Muir

3 Calming Our Bodies

Our bodies know when we are stressed long before our minds tell us. Muscle tension is our bodies' way of letting us know that we are stressed. Without realizing it, we tense our bodies when we experience stress. When the stress stops, the tension goes away.

Most of the time, we are too busy to tune into what's happening in our bodies. We wait until we are hurting or sick. Our bodies are very wise. We just have to listen to what our bodies are trying to tell us about how we feel.

Inside/outside exercise

You can try this three-step exercise by yourself. You can also have fun doing it with someone else. Take turns telling each other what you notice about yourselves—inside and outside.[3]

Two-Minute Stress-Busters

Sing a song.

Dance a jig.

Sip a cup of tea.

Play a drum.

Pet a dog.

✤ **food for thought**

For fast-acting relief, slow down.

—Lily Tomlin

STEP 1: Notice what is around you—your **outside** world. Say what you are aware of. "I notice...the cars going by outside the room, papers moving, the light on the leaves, the brown floor."

STEP 2: Now notice what is happening **inside** your body—your inside world. Say what you become aware of. "I notice...feeling warm, I hear ringing...in my head, in my mind I see a...favourite place of mine."

STEP 3: Move back and forth between noticing things inside and outside your body. "I am aware...of the chair pressing against my leg (inside world)... the blue wall (outside world)... my shoulders hunching up (inside world)... people talking outside the door (outside world)..."

Do this at different times during the day. This exercise will help you to become more aware of what your body is feeling. You will begin to notice all kinds of things—inside and out. If you keep a journal, write about what you noticed.

Letting-go-of-tension exercise

When you feel tense, try this exercise.[4] Most of us do not realize that our muscles are tight all the time. This is a way of telling the difference between being tense and relaxed. All you need to do is relax groups of muscles in your body, one group at a time. Here's how you do it.

STEP 1: Find a quiet place. No one should bother you for about 15 minutes. Turn down the lights. Sit in a comfortable chair. You can close your eyes or keep them open. If you like to keep your eyes open, look gently down towards your heart. Rest your hands on your lap or put your arms on the sides of the chair. The most important thing is to be comfortable.

STEP 2: Check how your body feels before you begin the exercise.

STEP 3: Take a few slow, deep breaths.

STEP 4: For each part of your body, breathe in and tighten a muscle group for a count of 5. When you breathe out, tell yourself to "relax" and let the tension go. Imagine the tension melting away in the warm sun. Tense and relax in this order:

- Bend both arms at the elbows.
- Make a fist with each hand. Tighten. Relax.

- Press your back against the chair. Relax.
- Tighten your belly area. Relax.
- Stretch out your lower legs and tighten. Relax.
- Tighten your jaw. Relax.
- Squeeze your eyes shut. Relax.
- Pull your chin into your chest. Relax.
- Continue to breathe slowly and deeply.
- Notice your body feeling more relaxed.
  Let your body go limp like a rag doll.
- Slowly open your eyes if they were closed.

✤ **food for thought**

Freeing the body...

leads to freeing the heart.

—Gabrielle Roth

Do you notice a difference from when you started the exercise?

Eating well

The right food makes us feel good. The wrong food makes us feel more stressed. We know that buying all the right foods is expensive. Here are some tips for eating well and shopping on a budget.

...ng on a low budget.

d.

his is a bonus.

ve fun!

bles, in small amounts.

ın be kept on the shelf
are rice and pasta.

ke lentils. Other daring
ds of dried beans, which
ınd fibre. They are
s.

d in recipes
a carton.

ood buy.
fter the meat is cooked.

✤ **food for thought**

You can't always get the food you want, but you can do your best. Choose from these food groups:

- fruits and vegetables
- whole-grain breads and cereals
- skim or 1 percent milk
- low-fat cheese and low-fat yogurt
- meats, chicken, and fish
- nuts and beans.

More tips for good health

✤ **food for thought**

You don't get ulcers from what you eat. You get them from what's eating you.

—Vicki Baum, writer

✔	Eat at regular times each day. Avoid skipping meals or going too long between meals. That's when we tend to overeat, or eat junk food.
✔	Drink lots of water between meals. Water makes up about 70 percent of our body weight. If you don't drink enough water, you can get headaches and feel stiff and tired. Try to drink about 8 glasses a day.
✔	Say "No!" to junk food. Junk food has lots of fat and sugar in it. Too much fat raises blood pressure, which also goes up when under stress.
✔	Cut down on the amount of salt you use. Salt causes high blood pressure. Packaged snack foods often have a lot of salt in them.
✔	Cut down on caffeine. We will talk about caffeine in the next section.
✔	Try one or two of these tips for two to three weeks. Then try another. You can change what you do a little bit at a time.

Shopping tips for healthy foods

The best time to buy fruits and vegetables is during their growing season. Here are the best times to shop for these in many parts of North America.[5]

When to buy healthy foods

Fruits and Vegetables	Best Time to Buy Them						
	May	*June*	*July*	*Aug.*	*Sept.*	*Oct.*	*Nov.*
asparagus	✓	✓					
beans			✓	✓	✓	✓	✓
broccoli		✓	✓	✓	✓		
cabbage			✓	✓	✓	✓	✓
corn			✓	✓	✓		
cucumbers			✓	✓	✓		
green peppers			✓	✓	✓		
lettuce		✓	✓	✓	✓		
peas		✓	✓	✓	✓		
rhubarb		✓	✓	✓			
strawberries		✓	✓	✓	✓		
tomatoes		✓	✓	✓	✓		
winter squash				✓	✓	✓	✓

Caffeine

Caffeine does a great job of making our bodies behave as if stressed. Our heart rate and blood pressure go way up. Our breathing becomes faster. We may have jittery feelings. We may feel anxious, fearful, or cranky. Do we really want to add this to feeling stressed?

Caffeine is a drug to which we can become addicted. We get headaches, and become sleepy and grumpy when we first quit drinking coffee, tea, or pop. We may also have trouble concentrating.

If you want to limit caffeine, do it slowly by cutting back about one third. If you drink nine cups of coffee, drink only six cups. Do this for a week. Then cut back some more for another week.

When coming to class to do the exam the next day, my nerves are on end. I'm nervous from too much coffee. My palms are sweaty. My mind goes blank sometimes. Time is of the essence. Time is running out. I'm constantly looking at my watch or at the clock on the wall, which is a waste of time. Finally time's up! I only hope I passed.

—Glen Dumont

Sleep

How often do we toss and turn at night because we are worried about something? Then, we become more worried and anxious because we aren't getting the sleep we need? Lack of sleep can cause us to feel anxious and stressed. It is important that we find ways to help us get a good night's sleep.

✤ **food for thought**

A good laugh and a long sleep are the best cures in the doctor's book.

—Irish Proverb

Do any of these things happen to you?[6]

Check the boxes that tell about you.

- ○ You often take more than an hour to get to sleep.
- ○ You wake up often in the night and have trouble getting back to sleep.
- ○ You wake up much too early and can't get back to sleep.
- ○ You need more than the usual amount of sleep each night. For example, you need 14 hours of sleep instead of 8.

If you checked any of the above, read on. You need to improve your sleep.

Tips for sleeping better

✤ **food for thought**

When you feel dog tired at night, it may be because you've growled all day long.

—Unknown

Check off the ideas you think you'd like to try. Can you think of any other ideas to share? Keep a sleep journal. Track those ideas that work best for you.

✓	Try not to drink alcohol before going to sleep. Drinking may make you sleepy, but it doesn't let you sleep well. You will wake up often during the night.
✓	Pick a time to go to bed and stick to it every night. Try to stay on the same schedule even on weekends, especially if you are depressed.
✓	Do you like to stay up late but want to start going to bed earlier? Make the change slowly. Say you go to bed at midnight and want to go to sleep at 10 p.m. Go to bed half an hour earlier for a week. Then the next week, go to bed half an hour earlier again.

✓	Get up the same time every day, even if you feel you want to sleep in. The sleep you get in the early morning doesn't do a lot for you. You are better to get up.
✓	Save your bedroom for sleep. Do all your other activities somewhere else. Working, eating, reading an exciting book, talking on the phone, and watching TV are better done in another room.
✓	Sleep with the right temperature in your room. From 65 to 69° F (18 to 21° C) is best. Some people like it cooler.
✓	Sleep in a quiet room. In a noisy neighbourhood, use earplugs or hang cloth over the windows to help make it quieter.
✓	Take short naps or no naps in the day. To help you sleep at night, take naps less than 20 minutes long.
✓	Get your body ready to sleep. At least one hour before going to bed it is best to avoid • large meals • being in bright light • lots of exercise.
✓	Practice breathing to quiet your mind. Often people go to bed thinking about their problems, or planning the next day. Before bed, let the mind rest. Focusing on your breathing can help you sleep. It relaxes your body and helps the mind settle down and be quiet. Try one of the breathing exercises when you go to bed.

Physical exercise

Do you know?[7]

- People who don't do much physical activity are more likely to be depressed and anxious.
- People who are depressed and begin to be physically active improve their moods.
- People who have had depression and are exercising regularly are less likely to slip back into depression.
- Exercise can be a huge help for those with panic, anxiety, and post-traumatic stress disorder.
- Regular physical exercise helps people manage stressful life events with less distress.

✤ **food for thought**

If people concentrated on the really important things in life, there'd be a shortage of fishing poles.

—Doug Larson

But I don't have time to exercise!!! In fact, exercise saves time. Think of all the time lost when you couldn't sleep, felt too tired to work in the day, or couldn't stay focused. Exercise helps us feel better and sleep better.

What kind of exercise is good?

It doesn't matter so much what we do. It is more important that we do it. It's good if we choose exercise that we like to do. Many people enjoy more active sports such as biking, drumming, or dancing. Others like yoga or walking.

✤ **food for thought**

The most basic, fundamental tool of magic is the body.

—Vicki Noble

Physical exercise gives us more energy, which helps us do more. This helps us feel better, which brings us more energy to do more and feel better. It is like putting our money into a good savings program. It just keeps getting better and better.

✤ **food for thought**

Those who think they have no time for bodily exercise will sooner or later have to find time for illness.

—Edward Stanley

Exercise is a good way to get rid of stress that we have been holding. If we don't exercise on a regular basis, we don't release our stress and tension. We keep storing the stress in our body. When our body can't hold it anymore, we become sick. If we exercise 3 to 4 times a week for about 30 minutes each time, we will be in a better mood. We'll feel less anxious about things.

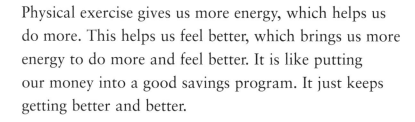

Although there are lots of ways for us to exercise, some are not easy to do. It costs money to join a fitness club. Some activities need expensive equipment. There is one thing we can do whenever we want. We just have to dress for the weather and take a step out the door. Walk!

Tips to get started with walking.[8]

✓	Avoid doing too much at the beginning. The first week, walk out your door, walk for 10 minutes, and go home again.
✓	You can make your walk a little longer each week. Just add five minutes each week.
✓	Walk tall. This helps you breathe more easily and is less tiring. Check to make sure your shoulders are relaxed.
✓	Drink lots of water before you go walking. Drink during your walk and afterwards.
✓	Get into a habit of walking at the same time every day, on certain days of the week. A routine helps you stick to your action plan for being less stressed.
✓	Go with a friend if you like company. If you want company but don't feel like talking, offer to walk your neighbour's dog.
✓	If you have concerns about your health, check with your doctor first about your walking plan.

Notice that the way your body feels changes your mood and your breath. A relaxed body brings a calm mind and a peaceful breath. Pick one of the calming body activities to start with. Notice the difference it makes after a few weeks. Our bodies take care of us. We need to take care of our bodies.

✤ **food for thought**

Go for how you feel, not for how you look.

4 Calming Our Breath

Breathing exercises help us relax. They help us learn more about what is happening in our bodies. Paying attention to breathing helps our minds become calm and rested. Breathing the right way also helps slow down our jittery thoughts. Breathing exercises are easy. They don't cost anything, and we can do them anywhere we go.

We need to breathe properly to take in oxygen and get rid of old, stale air. If we don't breathe properly, stressful times become even harder. When we are stressed, our breathing becomes faster. We breathe more into our chest than our belly. Chest-breathing makes us feel more anxious and afraid. Breathing properly will calm our minds, and our bodies will relax.

Learning to breathe into our bellies will help us feel less anxious. We knew how to do this when we were babies.

Two-Minute Stress-Busters

Watch a sunset.

Blow bubbles.

Do yoga.

Take a few deep breaths.

Listen to your breath.

As we grew up, we have forgotten how to do this. Belly-breathing is an easy way to bring on the **relaxation response.**

Belly-breathing

To begin, we want to find out where our breath goes in our bodies. Try this exercise.[10]

STEP 1: Close your eyes. Put one hand on your belly, right below your waist, and put your other hand on your chest, right in the centre.

STEP 2: Without trying to change your breathing, notice how you are breathing. Which hand rises the most as you take a breath in? Is it the hand on your chest, or the hand on your belly?

✤ **food for thought**

Everything you do, the pace you keep, the feelings you have, and the choices you make are influenced by the rhythm... of your breath.

—Donna Farhia

Next, practice breathing into your belly. Try this.

STEP 1: On your back, lie on a rug or blanket on the floor. Your legs can be straight or you can bend your knees. Choose the position that is most comfortable for you. Your arms are at your sides, a little bit away from your body. Your palms are facing up. You can close your eyes or open them a little bit. Relax your eyes.

STEP 2: Notice your breathing as you breathe in and out. Place one of your hands on the spot that seems to rise and fall the most as you breathe.

STEP 3: Gently place both of your hands or a book on your belly. Notice your breathing. Notice how your belly rises with each breath. As you breathe out, your belly falls.

STEP 4: Breathe through your nose.

Is your chest moving with your belly, or is it still?
Spend a minute or two noticing how your belly moves.

You can also do this lying on your stomach. Rest your forehead on your folded hands. Take deep belly-breaths so you can feel your belly pushing against the floor.

Breath-counting

This exercise will help slow down your breath.[11] It will also calm and relax your mind.

STEP 1: Sit or lie in a comfortable position with your arms and legs uncrossed. Keep your spine straight.

STEP 2: Breathe deeply into your belly. Just let your breath happen. Take easy, gentle breaths.

STEP 3: As you breathe out, count '1' to yourself. As you keep on breathing in and out, count each breath out: "2...3...4..."

STEP 4: Once you have counted to four, do the same thing over and over again for about 5 minutes. Can someone time it for you? Maybe you can take turns with a friend or tutor.

STEP 5: Notice your breathing getting slower, your body relaxing, and your mind calming as you practice this exercise.

You can do this exercise before writing an exam, waiting to see the doctor, or before an interview—anytime you feel anxious or worried.

✤ **food for thought**

Fear less, hope more; Eat less, chew more; Whine less, breathe more; Talk less, say more; Love more, and all good things will be yours.

—Swedish Proverb

The relaxing sigh[12]

When you yawn or sigh, it means that you are not getting enough air into your body. This can make you feel more tense. Sighing and yawning help you breathe

in more air. A sigh helps you let go of tension. You can practice sighing whenever you need to so you can relax. This is fun when you do it with other people. You will laugh and that brings more air into your body.

STEP 1: Sit or stand up straight.

STEP 2: Let out a big sigh, letting out a big sound as you do it.

STEP 3: Feel the relief as you breathe out with a loud sigh.

STEP 4: Continue to sigh for 8 to 12 times. Let yourself feel more and more relaxed as you do.

STEP 5: Repeat whenever you feel the need for it.

✤ **food for thought**

Breathing in, I calm body and mind

Breathing out, I smile

—Thich Nhat Hanh

Gentle breath

STEP 1: Lie on your back with your knees bent. You can also sit comfortably in a chair.

STEP 2: Imagine that you can breathe into all parts of your body to relax it.

STEP 3: Begin by breathing in and out with slow easy breaths.

STEP 4: As you breathe in, say to yourself, "I breathe in peace and calmness." Picture your body feeling light as you breathe in peace.

STEP 5: When you breathe out, say "I breathe out all tension and worry." Picture your body letting go of all tension. Feel it softening.

STEP 6: Continue gently breathing in and out for a few minutes to allow yourself to open and relax.

Breathing the right way helps us relax. It also helps improve our memories and abilities to focus, which makes it easier to learn.

✤ **food for thought**

I need to take an emotional breath, step back, and remind myself who's actually in charge of my life.

—Judith M. Knowlton

5 Calming Our Minds

When a stressful event happens, what are your first thoughts? The way you think about a stressful event can make you feel even more stressed. Are you a person who thinks that whatever happens, it's someone else's fault? Do you say to yourself that it's something that you can't do anything about? Or do you look at the stressful event as a challenge? Do you say it's an opportunity to learn something about yourself? Do you think the event could make you stronger?

We can change how we think about stressful things. Our thinking can help us—or do us in. Our minds control our emotions. If we think sad thoughts, we feel unhappy. If we think anxious thoughts, we become tense. When we think that we are going to be lonely and unhappy, chances are we will. This chapter will help us relax our minds and change how we think.

Two-Minute Stress-Busters

Write in a journal.

Light a candle.

Ask for what you need.

Say something nice to someone.

Laugh out loud.

Tell a joke.

Visualization

✤ **food for thought**

Try this!

Every day when you wake up,
say to yourself 20 times
"Every day, in every way,
I am getting better and better."

—Emile Coue

We can feel less stressed by using our imaginations. It's called the **power of positive thinking.** Even when we are not relaxed, we can imagine relaxation spreading through our bodies. We can imagine ourselves in a safe and beautiful place. This place can be one we know, or one we make up. If we imagine we are relaxed, we will feel relaxed.

Creating your special place

Create your own special place in your imagination.[13] Dream of a place where you can go anytime to relax. This place may be indoors or out.

Have someone slowly read the passage below.
Or, read it first to yourself.

To go to your special place, lie down so that you are comfortable. Close your eyes or if you prefer, look softly down toward your heart.... Imagine yourself walking slowly to a quiet place in your mind.... Your place can be indoors or outside.... It needs to be peaceful and safe.... Picture yourself leaving your worries behind.... Notice the view in the distance....

What do you see?.... What do you hear?.... What do you smell?.... Notice what is in front of you.... Make the temperature comfortable.... Be safe here.... Look around for a special spot, a private spot.... Find the path to this place.... Feel the ground with your feet.... Look above you.... What do you see?...hear?...smell?.... Walk down this path until you can enter your own quiet, comfortable, safe place.

You have arrived at your special place.... What is under your feet?.... How does it feel?.... Take several steps.... What do you

✤ **food for thought**

God, grant me the serenity to accept the things I cannot change, the courage to change the things I can, and the wisdom to know the difference.

– a soldier's prayer from the 14th century

see above you?.... What do you hear?.... Do you hear something else?.... Reach and touch something....What is its texture?.... Are there pens, paper, paints nearby, or is there sand to draw in and clay to play with?.... Go to them, handle them, feel them. These are your special tools to reveal ideas or feelings to you...

✤ **food for thought**

The world of reality has its limits; the world of imagination is boundless.

—Jean-Jacques Rousseau

Sit or lie in your special place.... Notice its smells...sound... sights.... This is your place and nothing can harm you here.... If danger is here, get rid of it.... You are alone and safe here. No one can come here unless invited.... Now spend 3 to 5 minutes feeling relaxed, safe, and comfortable.

Remember the smells, tastes, sights, sounds of this place.... You can come back and relax here whenever you want.... Leave by the same path.... Notice the ground, touch things near you.... Look far away and take in the view.... Remind yourself that you can come to this special place whenever you wish. Say to yourself, "I can relax here," or "This is my special place. I can come here whenever I wish."

If you can't see anything, that is fine. Just notice the nice feelings in your body as you relax.

Now open your eyes and spend a little while enjoying being relaxed.

You can write about your special place in your journal.

Changing self-talk

Almost all day, we talk to ourselves inside our heads. What do you say to yourself? Do you ever say, "What a dummy," to yourself when you have done something wrong? Maybe you say, "I'm so stupid!" when you've dropped something, or have forgotten to do something. When you say these things to yourself, it makes you tense and stressed. If you say these things often enough, you begin to believe them.

We say things that make us feel bad about ourselves. Most of the time we don't even know that we are doing it. Sometimes others put us down and we begin to believe what they say. These are called "put-downs." Others put us down, and we begin to believe them.

Below, write the answers to these questions or tell someone:

When do you feel bad about yourself? Why does this happen? Who is with you?

✤ **food for thought**

To be at peace with ourselves, we need to know ourselves.

—Caitlin Matthews

What kinds of things would you like to do? Have you stopped yourself from trying because you thought you couldn't do them very well?

____

____

____

____

____

____

✤ **food for thought**

I want to sing like the birds sing, not worrying who hears or what they think.

—Rumi

Now try changing your self-talk.

STEP 1: In box 1, on page 63, write about a time this week when you felt bad.

STEP 2: In box 2, write what you said to yourself when you felt bad.

STEP 3: In box 3, write something good that you would rather say.

The second row of boxes show you an example.

The ways I talk to myself

Whenever you notice you are thinking bad things about yourself, switch to a good thought.

Box 1	Box 2	Box 3
What I was doing. I made some spelling mistakes in my writing class.	**What I said to myself.** I'm so stupid. I never get anything right.	**If I am my own best friend, this is what I'd say.** I can learn to spell better. It's OKAY for me to make mistakes.

Thought-stopping[14]

This activity helps you get rid of the worrying you do every day.

STEP 1: "Hold" the worrying thought that you are thinking about.

STEP 2: Close your eyes and focus on the thought.

STEP 3: Count to three.

STEP 4: Shout out loud "Stop!" If others are around you, say "Stop!" just to yourself. Or, imagine a huge STOP sign or a flashing red light.

STEP 5: If the worrying thought comes back, do steps 1 to 4 again.

STEP 6: Go back to what you were doing before the thought came.

Here are some things you can do next:

- Focus on what you were doing before the thought came.
- Think about something good happening to you.
- Get busy.
- Say: "It's not helpful. I don't want to worry anymore."

Journal of good things

Our self-esteem improves when we say good things about ourselves. If one good saying helps, try more.

In a journal, write down all the good things that you did in a week. You can also write down all the good things people have said to you, or done for you. A good time to do this is just before you go to bed at night. You will go to sleep thinking positive thoughts about yourself. If you keep doing this every night, your list will get longer and longer.

✤ **food for thought**

Your voice takes you to your heart.

—Gabrielle Roth

You can also list all the good qualities and skills you have. One person wrote this list:

- I am friendly.
- I can play pool well.
- I can tell a good story.
- I am helpful, especially with other students in my literacy program.

Post your list on the wall where you can see it every day. Then read it aloud to yourself until you know it by heart. Keep adding to your list as you think of more ideas. Soon you will know this in your head, and you won't need the list anymore.

Practicing for stressful times

Think of a situation or activity that is coming up for you. It could be anything that you will be nervous about. For example, think of telling a friend that you don't like something she does. Or you might be getting ready to write a test. Picture yourself feeling calm and relaxed in that situation.

STEP 1: Close or lower your eyes and take a few calm, slow breaths. Picture tension leaving your body. Take 1 or 2 minutes to do this.

STEP 2: Imagine yourself doing the activity, whatever it is.

STEP 3: Focus on feeling relaxed while you picture yourself doing it.

STEP 4: Imagine the place where you are doing it. Who is there? What are they doing? What does the place look like? What are you wearing?

STEP 5: Picture yourself being very calm and relaxed as you do the activity.

STEP 6: Imagine something good that will happen afterwards.

Practice this 2 times a day for 5 minutes each time. The best time is when your mind is relaxed. Try it when you first wake up in the morning, right after you do one of the breathing exercises. You can also do it when you go to bed at night, just before you fall asleep.

> I have chosen to visit my mother more often, but for shorter periods of time. This way, the time I spend will have more quality and I can leave when my anxiety overwhelms me. My dad visits her every day, feeds her every meal, changes all her diapers and gives her medication that is not taken orally. He is my hero and defines the commitment of marriage. My mom will never die alone, that gives me some comfort.
>
> –Jennifer Ellenwood

Meditating

Meditating is a way to quiet our bodies and minds. We can focus on one thing. It can be a word, a sound, or group of words, called a **mantra.**

We can focus on an object like a candle flame or a flower. We can focus on our breathing. We can focus on anything. We do this so that our minds become more still and quiet. Our thinking slows down when our minds are relaxed. We find the quiet that is within us. We feel at peace.

When our minds focus on something like our breathing, we can't think of anything else. Meditating helps with anxiety, depression, and anger. Meditating works best if we do a little every day.

✤ **food for thought**

Some examples of mantras that you can say:

- "Relax" or "peace"
- "I am calm."
- The sound "OM"

How to meditate

Getting ready to meditate

STEP 1: Find a time to meditate that is best for you. To begin, start with 2 to 5 minutes of meditating. When you feel more comfortable, you can work up to 15 to 20 minutes a day.

STEP 2: Be comfortable. You can sit in a chair with your back straight and your head relaxed. Or you can sit on a pillow on the floor with your legs crossed in front of you. If you lie down, you might fall asleep instead of meditating.

STEP 3: Close your eyes. If that doesn't feel OKAY for you, look gently down towards your heart. Breathe evenly and smoothly.

STEP 4: Notice where your body feels tense or tight. Each time you breathe out, imagine those areas softening and relaxing.

STEP 5: Notice where your breath wants to go in your body. When you breathe in, is it up high in your chest? Is it down low in your belly? Feel your belly fill up as the air goes in. It will relax as the breath goes out.

✤ **food for thought**

The time to relax is when you don't have time for it.

—Sydney J. Harris

Beginning to meditate

As you breathe out, say a word to yourself, such as "peace" or "relax." Or focus on an object, such as a candle flame. If you begin to think of other things, gently let the thoughts go. Bring your attention back to your breath, word, or object.

Get ready to stop meditating. Stretch your body a little or sit quietly for a few minutes.

Breath-counting meditation[15]

Following the breath in and out helps us feel peaceful and rested.

STEP 1: Sit in a comfortable position.

STEP 2: Take a few deep breaths. Either close your eyes or look on a spot on the floor about 4 feet in front of you.

STEP 3: Take deep, but not forced breaths into your belly. As you do, focus your attention on each part of the breath: the breath in, the moment in between breaths, the breath out, the moment in between breaths.

STEP 4: As you breathe out, say '1.' Keep on counting each outward breath: '2...3...4.' When you get to '4', start at '1' again. If you lose count, simply start over.

STEP 5: When your mind wanders, gently go back to the counting of your breath.

You can change your thinking to feel better about yourself. Most of the exercises here can be done anytime—such as when you are waiting in line at the bus stop, or at a grocery store. Even for a short time, the more you practice, the more you find yourself smiling. You will feel less stressed and have more energy.

✤ **food for thought**

Be content with what you have; rejoice in the way things are. When you realize there is nothing lacking, the whole world belongs to you.

—Lao Tzu

Remember, the best exercise is the one that works for you.

You can try different combinations of exercises to calm the body, mind, and breath. For example, you can do the Letting-Go-of-Tension exercise first. Then you can do Breath-Counting. Follow that by meditating right before you go to bed. After you try different exercises, write the ones you like best the circles below.

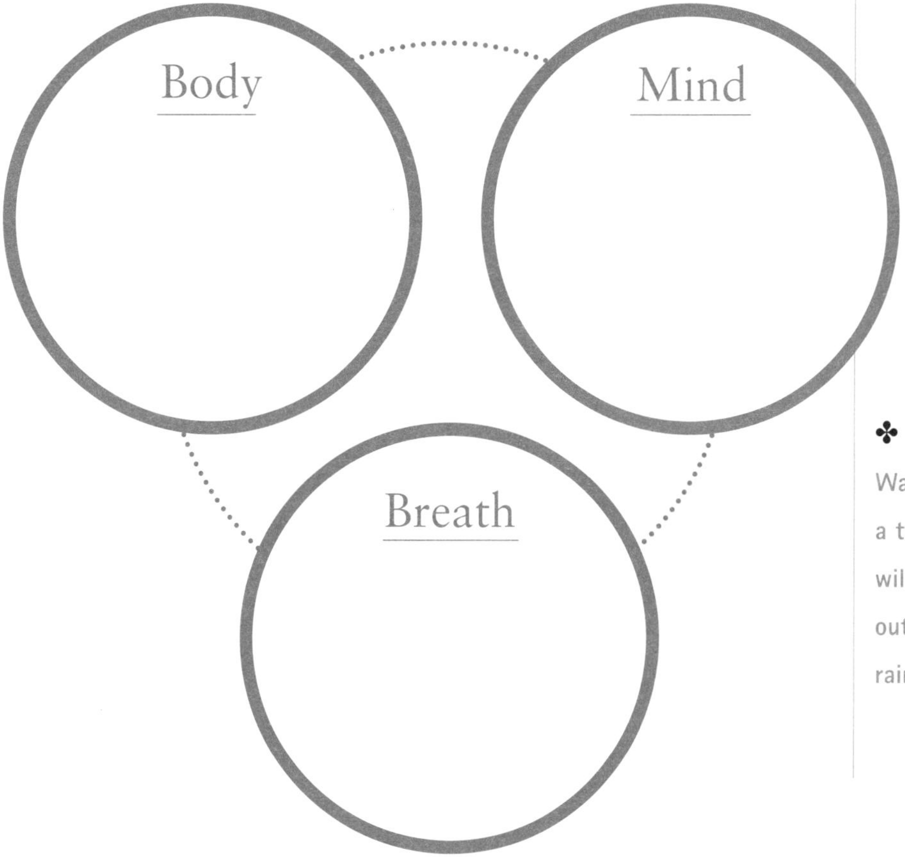

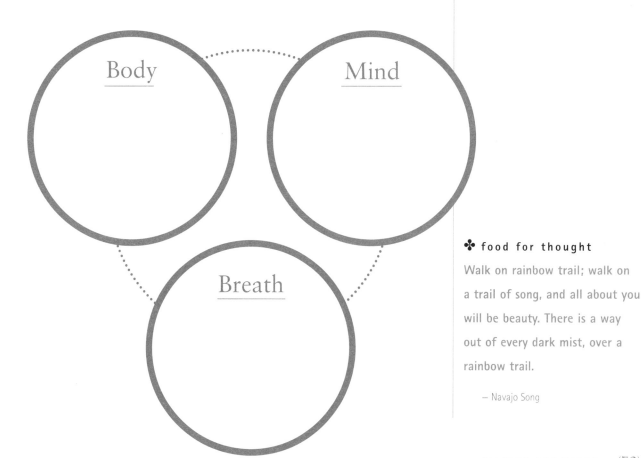

food for thought

Walk on rainbow trail; walk on a trail of song, and all about you will be beauty. There is a way out of every dark mist, over a rainbow trail.

– Navajo Song

COUNSELLING SERVICE

6 Dealing with Too Much Stress

Sometimes stress builds up. It's too much to manage by ourselves. Then it's a good idea to talk to someone. Tell a doctor, a counselor or health worker about how you feel. This section talks about three different ways stress can affect you.

✤ **food for thought**

There is more to life than increasing its speed.

—Mohandas K. Gandhi

Panic and Anxiety

What do panic and anxiety feel like in our bodies?

A panic or anxiety attack begins without any warning or idea of why it is starting. You will know if you are having a panic attack—you feel very much afraid. The feelings are stronger than if you are just feeling anxious or "stressed."

When people have a panic attack they may

- breathe very quickly
- not be able to get enough breath
- feel the heart beating very fast
- sweat more than usual
- shake or tremble
- choke and have a tight feeling in the chest
- feel sick to the stomach and be dizzy
- think they are having a heart attack.

During a panic attack, we may also have trouble connecting with other people. We may avoid places or events where we think we might have an attack. We may stop doing activities that have a lot of people around—like going to school or taking the bus. We begin to limit what we do and where we go. Other things begin to happen. If we are afraid to go out in public, our self-esteem may drop.

✤ **food for thought**

Over four million Americans suffer from panic attacks, according to the National Institute of Mental Health. That number is about 5% of the adult American population. Many researchers feel that even this number is a *low estimate...*

—The Anxiety Network International

What can we do about it?

We can treat panic anxiety by learning what it is and what causes it. We can also imagine what our lives would be like without panic attacks. We can learn what to do so they don't happen again.

Learning relaxed breathing helps calm your nervous system. Change your breathing. Your emotions will calm down and your body will relax. You want to breathe as a baby breathes. If you watch a baby breathe, you will see the baby's whole body breathe. This is what we should do all the time. If you haven't breathed this way for a while, you will need to practice each day in order for it to feel natural.

Two-minute natural breathing

It helps to practice natural breathing each day. You can do this at anytime—during breaks or waiting in line.

STEP 1: Gently and slowly breathe in a normal amount of air through your nose. Fill your lower belly only.

STEP 2: Breathe out easily.

✤ **food for thought**

Smile, breathe, and go slowly.

—Thich Nhat Hanh

Calming Counts[16]

STEP 1: Sit comfortably.

STEP 2: Take a long, deep breath and breathe out slowly while saying the word "relax" to yourself.

STEP 3: Close your eyes, if you are OKAY with doing that. If not, look down gently towards your heart.

STEP 4: Let yourself take 10 natural, easy breaths. With each 'out' breath, count down, starting with '10.'

STEP 5: On your next out breath, count '9.'

When you breathe in, notice any tensions, perhaps in your jaw or forehead or stomach. Imagine those tensions becoming softer.

STEP 6: When you reach the number '1,' open your eyes again.

Take a moment to notice what you are feeling.
Ask yourself these questions:

- What do I notice?
- What has changed for me?
- How do I feel right now?
- Does my body feel relaxed?

Did you feel some of your muscles relax? Is your breathing calmer? If you said yes to either question, you are learning about controlling your tension.

Four Steps to Calmness[17]

STEP 1: When you begin to feel upset, ask yourself these questions:

- How likely is this event or situation to happen?
- Do you think it will happen for sure?
- Do you think it might happen?
- Do you think there is a slim chance of it happening?
- Or do you think it may not happen at all?

STEP 2: Think, What would be the worst thing that could happen if this event took place. How awful would it be? Try not to exaggerate your answer.

STEP 3: Make up a plan so that the event you fear doesn't happen. Or a plan to keep it from happening the way you think. This helps you be more realistic about the event.

STEP 4: Plan how you would cope if the event you fear did happen. Focus on the actions you **would** take instead of fearing the event itself.

✤ **food for thought**

Life is not a problem to be solved, but a mystery to be lived.

—Thomas Morton

Use the spaces below to write your Calmness Plan in a few sentences or phrases. Write the plan on a card to carry with you as a reminder. Whenever you begin to worry about the event, read your card to know that you have a good plan.

My Calmness Plan

The event I am anxious about

____

How likely is it to happen?

____

This is what I can do to prevent the event. Or, here's what I can do to stop it from happening the way I fear.

____

____

If the event **does** happen, here's how I will cope.

____

____

So What.. and So What If?

Do you find yourself thinking, "What if...such and such happens?" You will become anxious when you think this way. While you never find the answer, you may keep thinking this way. It makes you worry even more.[18]

Are you a "What if?" thinker? You can change what you say to yourself. Don't think, **"What if** I sneeze during the interview?" Think, **"So what** if I sneeze during the interview?" Change "What if I become anxious?" to "So what if I become anxious?" "What if...?" thinking stresses your body. "So what if...?" helps you to be calm.

✤ **food for thought**

Worry is like a rocking chair,
it will give you something to do,
but it won't get you anywhere.

—Unknown

Think of some "What if's...?" you say to yourself or to others. Change them to a "So what if's..."

What if....	So what if...

Burnout

Burnout develops over time. It happens when we keep trying to meet a goal that cannot be reached. We keep thinking we can do it, and we work harder to get there. We feel as if we have too much to do. There is no end in sight of the work facing us. The stress response has gone on for too long.

✤ **food for thought**

No one can get inner peace by pouncing on it.

—Harry Emerson Fosdick

We first start feeling burnout when we are tired and feel alone. We become impatient and begin to resent doing this work. We lose the excitement we had when we first started. After a while we find we don't care about the work, but we keep trying even harder to meet our goals. When we reach this point, it is a good idea to see what changes we can make. Take a good break from what we are doing.

The Burnout Checklist

Do you think you might be suffering from burnout? Check the boxes that tell about your life.[19]

- ○ Do you get tired easily? Do you feel worn out?
- ○ Do you get upset when people tell you, "You don't look so good lately"?
- ○ Are you working harder and harder but feel as if you're getting nothing done?
- ○ Are you more disappointed in the world around you?
- ○ Are you sad a lot and don't know why?
- ○ Are you more forgetful (missing doctor visits, losing things)?
- ○ Are you grumpy? More short-tempered? Do you expect more and more from the people around you?
- ○ Are you spending less time with your friends and family?
- ○ Do you always feel bad, or are you sick all the time?
- ○ Do you feel confused at the end of the day?
- ○ Do you have trouble feeling happy?
- ○ Are you unable to laugh at a joke about yourself?
- ○ Does sex seem like more trouble than it's worth?
- ○ Do you have very little to say to people?

Tips to help with burnout

✓	Be with people. Make new friends or connect with old ones. Learn to talk about your feelings.
✓	Make a positive change. Try to change the way you are working. Think about giving up that second job. Ask a relative to help with the children.
✓	Talk to your boss about changing a deadline, or get your spouse to do more of the family driving.
✓	Notice what makes you most tense. Work to reduce that tension.
✓	Begin to nurture yourself first, before looking after everyone else.
✓	Say "No!" Turn down people who ask you to do more.
✓	Back off from doing everything yourself. Ask others to help you do things.
✓	Think about what really matters to you. Stick by this.
✓	Pace yourself. You have only so much energy. Spread your energy on what is important to you. Bring in more fun, love, and relaxation.
✓	Try to worry less.
✓	Keep your sense of humour. Laugh a lot.

Post-Traumatic Stress Disorder

✤ **food for thought**

I try to take one day at a time, but sometimes several days attack me at once.

—Jennifer Yane

Post-Traumatic Stress Disorder (PTSD) can happen to anyone who has seen a terrible event. People can also have PTSD if something very scary happened to them. Things that can cause PTSD include:

- natural disasters such as floods, hurricanes, and tornadoes
- terrorist activities
- war
- personal attacks such as rape or childhood abuse
- residential school experiences.

✤ **food for thought**

PTSD will affect approximately 1 in 12 people at some point in their lives. Twice as many women as men develop the disorder, although the reasons for this are unclear.

—BC Partners for Mental Health and Addictions Information

Not everyone who has experienced or witnessed a violent event develops PTSD. Some have symptoms right after the event, but they go away. Others have symptoms for the rest of their lives.

People with PTSD relive the event. They have nightmares and flashbacks. Flashbacks are memories or nightmares about the event.

People with PTSD also have trouble with:

- sleeping
- relating to people
- depression
- addictions
- forgetting things
- partner relationships
- doing schoolwork.

PTSD often affects the body. These problems include:

- headaches
- stomach problems
- dizziness
- chest pains
- being sick more often than other people.

When should you see the doctor?

Look at the column to the right. If you have noticed some of these things, call your doctor for help.

Check off any items in the column if they are going on in your life.

- ○ You are anxious, nervous, cry a lot, or have trouble managing things.
- ○ You abuse alcohol or drugs to handle stress.
- ○ You have Post-Traumatic Stress Disorder.
- ○ You can't cope with a physical illness you have.
- ○ You blow up at family or friends for little reason.
- ○ You want to be alone all the time.

(7 Helping Our Children Live with Stress

What causes stress in our children?

Children feel stressed when big changes take place in their lives. Examples of these changes are:

- parents separating
- parents divorcing
- moving
- changing schools
- being taken away from the home
- seeing or experiencing abuse.

✤ **food for thought**

Whoever said you can't buy happiness, forgot little puppies.

—Gene Hill

Can you think of other things that can make children feel stressed? Write your answers below.

____

____

____

____

____

____

✤ **food for thought**

Kids as young as four can learn deep breathing and relaxation techniques. Do them together.

—CPAP Advocacy Report
Council of Provincial Associations of Psychologists

Below, name things that made you feel stressed when you were a child.

____

____

____

____

____

____

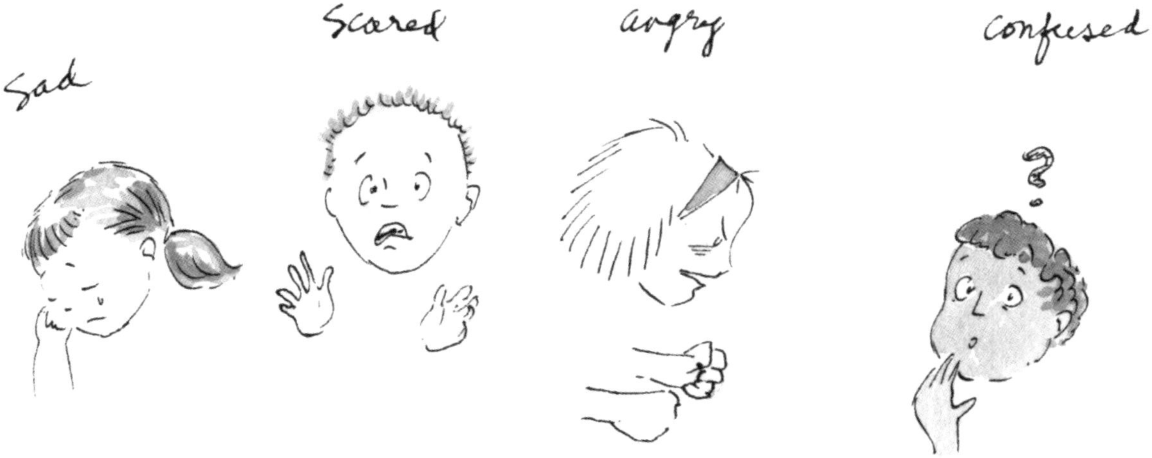

How do we know our children are stressed?*

Children show that they are stressed in many ways. Like adults, children have their limits. They can feel stressed whether it comes from good or bad things. If it is too much of a good or bad thing, it will affect how they feel and behave.

You can watch for changes in your children's behaviours. Notice if they begin acting like children a lot younger than they are. This is called **regression.**

✤ food for thought

Experience is a hard teacher. She gives you the test first; the lesson afterwards.

–Anonymous

*Adapted from PrepareRespondRecover.com. Retrieved May 11, 2005 from http://www.preparerespondrecover.com/childrensneeds/.

Different things bother children at different ages. Teenagers worry about their bodies as they grow up. Younger children in school may become very close to their pets. Children become very upset when their pets die.

Here are some examples of how children at different ages show stress.

Children's signs of stress at different ages

Ages 1 to 5	**Ages 5 to 11**
Cry without being able to stop.	Act younger than they are.
Shake with fear.	Have trouble sleeping.
Cling to someone more than normal.	Become frightened of bad weather.
Act as if they are a lot younger.	Get headaches and feel sick to the stomach.
Become very frightened of loud noises.	Refuse to go to school.
Become mixed up about things.	Fight with other children.
Change how much they eat or don't eat.	Want to be alone.
Wet the bed.	

Children's signs of stress at different ages

Ages 11 to 14	Ages 14 to 18
Be sad, depressed, suicidal. Show mean or hurtful behaviours. Become substance abusers. Like to be alone, without friends.	Get into trouble at school or with the police. Examples are stealing, acting out, picking fights. Sleep very long hours. Have nightmares. Become depressed.

What can we do to help?[20]

We can spend time listening and talking to our children. We can take time to do things with them, especially things they like to do.

✤ **food for thought**

Breathe. Let go. And remind yourself that this very moment is the only one you know you have for sure.

—Oprah Winfrey

✤ **food for thought**

What lies behind you and what lies before you are small matters compared to what lies within you.

—Unknown

Listening and doing

Listening	Doing
Listen quietly. Some children are able to sail though stressful times if they feel cared for.	Give children a place and time to tell about their fears and angers. They can do this by story telling, drawing or painting, making things and playing.
Comfort children so they feel safe.	Find things that your child likes to do. Do them together. Try walking to the park or taking a bike ride together.
Spend time with a child so there is time to talk.	Find time to do a hobby together.
Encourage children to talk about what upsets them.	Give lots of hugs and back rubs.
Help children use their imaginations. They can see in their minds special places they like to visit.	Show how to handle stress by example. They will learn by watching you.

References

1 Adapted from *Stress management* (1997), pp. 8-9. Pamphlet. Deerfield, MA: Channing L. Bete Co. Inc.

2 Adapted from Holes, T.H., & Rahe, R.H. (1967). *Social readjustment rating scale.* University of Washington School of Medicine.

3 Adapted from Davis, M., Eshelmann, E.R., & McKay, M. (2000). *The stress & relaxation reduction workbook* (5th ed.). Oakland, CA: New Harbinger Publications.

4 Adapted from American Institute for Preventive Medicine. (2005). *Success over stress* (5th ed.). [Pamphlet.] Farmington Hills, MI: American Institute for Preventive Medicine.

5 Adapted from Growing Alberta. (Summer 2000). *Food for thought magazine,* "Fresh from the market." Venture Publishing for Growing Alberta. Retrieved Summer 2000 from http://www.growingalberta.com/foodforthought.

6 Adapted from Paterson, R. & Bilsker, D. (2002). *Self-care depressions program patient guide.* Retrieved June 30, 2005 from http://www.randypaterson.com/SelfCareManual.pdf.

7 Adapted from Paterson, R. & Bilsker, D. (2002). *Self-care depressions program patient guide.* Retrieved June 30, 2005 from http://www.randypaterson.com/SelfCareManual.pdf.

8 Adapted from *The walking site: Beginning a fitness walking program.* Retrieved June 30, 2005 from http://www.thewalkingsite.com/beginner.html

9 Farhi, Donna. (1996). *The breathing book.* New York: Henry Holt and Company, LLC.

10 Adapted from Davis, M., Eschelmann, E.R., & McKay, M. (2000). *The stress & relaxation reduction workbook* (5th ed.). Oakland, CA: New Harbinger Publications.

11 Adapted from Davis, M., Eschelmann, E.R., & McKay, M. (2000). *The stress & relaxation reduction workbook* (5th ed.). Oakland, CA: New Harbinger Publications.

12 Adapted from Davis, M., Eschelmann, E.R., & McKay, M. (2000). *The stress & relaxation reduction workbook* (5th ed.). Oakland, CA: New Harbinger Publications.

13 Adapted from Davis, M., Eschelmann, E.R., & McKay, M. (2000). *The stress & relaxation reduction workbook* (5th ed.). Oakland, CA: New Harbinger Publications.

14 Adapted from American Institute for Preventive Medicine. (2005). *Success over stress* (5th ed.). [Pamphlet.] Farmington Hills, MI: American Institute for Preventive Medicine.

15 Adapted from Davis, M., Eschelmann, E.R., & McKay, M. (2000). *The stress & relaxation reduction workbook* (5th ed.). Oakland, CA: New Harbinger Publications.

16 Selection from DON'T PANIC: TAKING CONTROL OF ANXIETY ATTACKS by REID WILSON, PH.D. Copyright©1986 by R. Reid Wilson. Reprinted by permission of HarperCollins Publishers.

17 Selection from DON'T PANIC: TAKING CONTROL OF ANXIETY ATTACKS by REID WILSON, PH.D. Copyright©1986 by R. Reid Wilson. Reprinted by permission of HarperCollins Publishers.

18 Adapted from Peurifoy, R. Z. (1995). *Anxiety, phobias, & panic: A step-by-step program for regaining control of your life,* pp.148-149. Brentwood, TN: Warner Books.

19 Adapted from Johnson, D. *Awakenings: Burnout inventory.* Retrieved June 11, 2005 from http://www.lessonsforliving.com/burnout_inventory2 .

20 Adapted from Helping Children Manage Stress. Retrieved May 11, 2005 from http://www.extension.iastate.edu/Publications/PM1660F.pdf